This book belongs to:

_____

Let's Write

Donna McMillan

Vander Publishing House

Reginald and Tevin McMillan Graphic Artist

Reginald McMillan Graphics Designer

Copyright © 2013
ISBN-13: 978-0615882697 (Vander Publishing House)

ISBN-10: 0615882692

LET'S WRITE

A B C D E F
G H I J K L
M N O P Q
R S T U V W
X Y Z a b c d
e f g h i j k l
m n o p q r s
t u v w x y z

A New Beginning Preschool 2013

Let's Write

Aa

Apple

apricot

Bb

Banana

blackberries

Cc

Cherry

carrot

Dd

Dates

dewberry

Ee

Eggs

eggplant

Ff

Fish

fig

Gg

Grapes

grapefruit

Hh

Hotdog

hamburger

I i

Ice

ice cream

J j

Juice

jelly beans

K k

Ketchup

kiwi

L l

Lemon

lime

M m

Milk

mango

N n

Noodles

nuts

O o

Orange

onion

P p

Plum

pear

Q q

Quince

quiche

R r

Raspberry

rolls

S s

Strawberry

sandwich

T t

Tomato

turkey

U u

Ugli fruit

upside down cake

V v

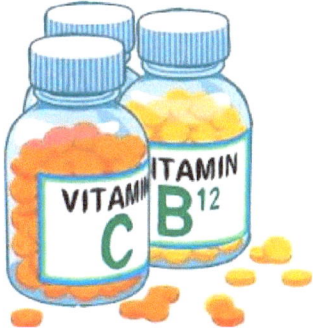

Vitamin

vegetables

W w

Watermelon

wheat

X x

Xipua

xiphias

Y y

Yogurt

yolk

Z z

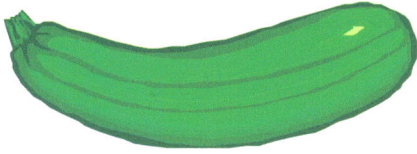

Zucchini

ziti

Given the right tools at the right time, no child will be left behind. This is the philosophy of Donna M. McMillan, a passionate, dedicated, and determined Early Childhood Education teacher. Donna was born and raised in the port city, Wilmington, North Carolina, where she obtained her Early Childhood Education Degree from Stanly Community College, and she also earned her Business Administration degree from Cape Fear Community College, respectively.

Donna is currently a pre-kindergarten teacher and she has committed her life to teaching each student to reach beyond their limits. She has developed her very own curriculum, which allows her to implement this concept. Parents speak highly of Donnas' personalized teaching style and of how her curriculum has contributed to their children entering into kindergarten with knowledge beyond that expected of a kindergartener. Donna ensures that she gives each student the tools they need to become not only successful students, but individuals as well.

Donna has several goals in life:

1. To reach as many children as possible.
2. To establish a community preschool where children are taught beyond what is expected of them at an early age.
3. To write several educational children books.

Donna has already begun working toward her third goal—writing children's books. The books will be integrated within her curriculum and also available for parents who aren't able to enroll their child into her program.

Ordinary preschool becomes extraordinary learning with Donna. She's truly mastered turning preschool education into a stepping stone for children to advance their knowledge and gain a true head-start in life!